Feel Good Now:

A Workbook Using THT

By Juniper Bartlett

Feel Good Now: A Workbook Using THT

Copyright © By Juniper Bartlett 2012-2017

First Printing, 2017

ISBN-13: 978-1546457442

This book is not intended to replace medical attention. Please do not stop taking any medications without the advice of your doctor.

Printed in the United States of America

Other books in this Series
By Juniper Bartlett:
Feel Good Now:
A Workbook Using EZDS

Feel Good Now:
A Workbook Using EZAS

Introduction

The doctor said that I think too much, so I gave it a lot of thought, studied different techniques, and developed Two Hands Touching, or THT.

THT is a way to access instant deep meditation, or instant deep relaxation. It can be used each morning to start your day off well. Use it any time you feel stressed, anxious, distracted, or find yourself thinking about things that don't make you happy. It can be used before a speech to calm your nerves, or before a test to help you focus.

THT can be used alone or with other techniques such as: positive affirmations; prayer; EZ Deletion Sequence; or visualization, so be creative. To use THT with other techniques, do THT, then remaining in same position, say your prayer, affirmation, etc..., then do THT again.

This guide will help you track your progress. It will give you a snapshot of your emotional wellbeing before the process and again after doing it for 21 days. When you are done with the process, you can start over, or simply continue to use it, knowing that you should feel better and better the longer you use it.

If you still feel like you need to get deeper, then move on to the next book: Feel Good Now: A Workbook Using EZDS. EZDS is for EZ Deletion Sequence, a technique that I developed to help people with deep seated issues such as affects of childhood trauma, feelings of unworthiness, etc...

This program is not intended to replace medical attention. Please do not stop taking any medications without your doctor's advice.

Warning: Do not do THT while driving or operating heavy equipment.

Please fill out this survey before starting this program. There is another one at the end so that you can compare how you feel before and after doing this program.

Please circle all that apply. I experience:

Anxiety-

Severity: 0 1 2 3 4 5 6 7 8 9 10

Frequency: Daily   Weekly   Monthly   Yearly

Stress-

Severity: 0 1 2 3 4 5 6 7 8 9 10

Frequency: Daily   Weekly   Monthly   Yearly

Depression-

Severity: 0 1 2 3 4 5 6 7 8 9 10

Frequency: Daily   Weekly   Monthly   Yearly

ADHD/ADD-

Severity: 0 1 2 3 4 5 6 7 8 9 10

Frequency: Daily   Weekly   Monthly   Yearly

Phobias/fears-: _____

Severity: 0 1 2 3 4 5 6 7 8 9 10

Frequency: Daily   Weekly   Monthly   Yearly

Insomnia-

Severity: 0 1 2 3 4 5 6 7 8 9 10

Frequency: Daily   Weekly   Monthly   Yearly

Irritability-

Severity: 0 1 2 3 4 5 6 7 8 9 10

Frequency: Daily   Weekly   Monthly   Yearly

Anger-

Severity: 0 1 2 3 4 5 6 7 8 9 10

Frequency: Daily   Weekly   Monthly   Yearly

Obsessive/negative thoughts-

Severity: 0 1 2 3 4 5 6 7 8 9 10

Frequency: Daily   Weekly   Monthly   Yearly

Mental/emotional breakdown-

Severity: 0 1 2 3 4 5 6 7 8 9 10

Frequency: Daily   Weekly   Monthly   Yearly

List of medications I currently take for these issues:

_____

_____

_____

_____

Notes:

_____

_____

_____

_____

_____

_____

_____

_____

_____

_____

_____

_____

Notes Continued:

_____

_____

_____

_____

_____

_____

_____

_____

_____

_____

_____

_____

_____

_____

_____

_____

_____

_____

_____

_____

_____

_____

_____

_____

Instructions for THT

Press the palms of your hands together and close your eyes. Ask yourself quietly in your mind, "What do my hands feel like?" Don't try to name the feelings, just feel the answer in your hands. Don't try to think or not think, just feel your hands. Do this until you feel a sense of peace in your heart and relaxed in your body, longer if you like. If your mind wanders, start over as many times as necessary.

THT for Sleep

Position yourself to go to sleep. Put all of your attention on your right hand. Then, put all of your attention on your left hand. Then, put all of your attention on both hands, keeping it there until you fall asleep. If your mind wanders, start over as many times as necessary.

THT with other techniques

Do THT, then, remaining in same position, say affirmation, prayer, etc..., then do THT again.

How To Use This Workbook

Do the first part of the daily exercises in the mornings, then the review parts in the evening. Do THT every morning. You can also do it throughout the day as needed and again in the evening if you would like. At least every morning is important

Some times that might be an especially good time to do THT are:

❖ Before a test
❖ Before an important meeting
❖ When you feel stress, anxiety, etc...
❖ When you get mad at someone
❖ When you don't like your thoughts
❖ When you have a craving
❖ While you are praying
❖ With affirmations
❖ Any reason you need it

Do THT for Sleep when you go to sleep to fall asleep faster, stay asleep longer and hopefully, have a good night's sleep.

Day 1

I control my thoughts; they don't control me.

Date:_____

AM

Last night, I slept (circle one)
Well   OK   Not well

I usually sleep (circle one) Well OK Not well

I take something to help me sleep (circle one)
Often Occasionally Rarely Never

Do THT in the morning,(Check here when done) ☐ then as needed throughout the day.

Affirmations I used with THT today:

_____

At the end of the day, take a moment to reflect on your day. Was it better than yesterday, the same or worse?_____

I needed to use THT today for

_____

I remembered to use it   Y   N

I felt more relaxed throughout the day than before this program   Y   N

I had less _____ today than before this program

Do THT in the evening. (Check here when done) ☐

Do THT for sleep if necessary.

Notes:

_____

_____

_____

_____

_____

_____

_____

_____

_____

_____

_____

_____

Day 2

If I don't like the thoughts that I think, then I can change them.

Date:_____

I needed THT for Sleep last night Y N

I remembered to use it   Y   N

I slept better than before this program Y N

Do THT in the morning,(Check here when done) ☐ then as needed throughout the day.

Affirmations I used with THT today:

_____

At the end of the day, take a moment to reflect on your day. Was it better than yesterday, the same or worse?_____

I needed to use THT today for

_____

I remembered to use it   Y   N

I felt more relaxed throughout the day than before this program   Y   N

I felt more relaxed throughout the day than before this program   Y   N

I had less _____ today than before this program

Do THT in the evening. (Check here when done) ☐

Do THT for sleep if necessary.

Notes:

_____

_____

_____

_____

_____

_____

_____

_____

_____

_____

_____

_____

_____

_____

Day 3

I can choose my thoughts.

Date:_____

I needed THT for Sleep last night Y N

I remembered to use it   Y   N

I slept better than before this program Y N

Do THT in the morning,(Check here when done) ☐ then as needed throughout the day.

Affirmations I used with THT today:

_____

At the end of the day, take a moment to reflect on your day. Was it better than yesterday, the same or worse?_____

I needed to use THT today for

_____

I remembered to use it   Y   N

I felt more relaxed throughout the day than before this program   Y   N

I felt more relaxed throughout the day than before this program   Y   N

I had less _____ today than before this program

Do THT in the evening. (Check here when done) ☐

Do THT for sleep if necessary.

Notes:

_____

_____

_____

_____

_____

_____

_____

_____

_____

_____

_____

_____

_____

_____

Day 4

We spend a lot of time with our thoughts; I choose ones I like.

Date:_____

I needed THT for Sleep last night Y N

I remembered to use it   Y   N

I slept better than before this program Y N

Do THT in the morning,(Check here when done) ☐ then as needed throughout the day.

Affirmations I used with THT today:

_____

At the end of the day, take a moment to reflect on your day. Was it better than yesterday, the same or worse?_____

I needed to use THT today for

_____

I remembered to use it   Y   N

I felt more relaxed throughout the day than before this program   Y   N

I felt more relaxed throughout the day than before this program   Y   N

I had less _____ today than before this program

Do THT in the evening. (Check here when done) ☐

Do THT for sleep if necessary.

Notes:

_____

_____

_____

_____

_____

_____

_____

_____

_____

_____

_____

_____

_____

_____

Day 5

My mind can be a battle field or Utopia or whatever I choose.

Date:_____

I needed THT for Sleep last night Y N

I remembered to use it   Y   N

I slept better than before this program Y N

Do THT in the morning,(Check here when done) ☐ then as needed throughout the day.

Affirmations I used with THT today:

_____

At the end of the day, take a moment to reflect on your day. Was it better than yesterday, the same or worse?_____

I needed to use THT today for

_____

I remembered to use it   Y   N

I felt more relaxed throughout the day than before this program   Y   N

I felt more relaxed throughout the day than before this program   Y   N

I had less _____ today than before this program

Do THT in the evening. (Check here when done) ☐

Do THT for sleep if necessary.

Notes:

_____

_____

_____

_____

_____

_____

_____

_____

_____

_____

_____

_____

_____

_____

Day 6

I am as powerful as I allow myself to believe.

Date:_____

I needed THT for Sleep last night Y N

I remembered to use it   Y   N

I slept better than before this program Y N

Do THT in the morning,(Check here when done) ☐ then as needed throughout the day.

Affirmations I used with THT today:

_____

At the end of the day, take a moment to reflect on your day. Was it better than yesterday, the same or worse?_____

I needed to use THT today for

_____

I remembered to use it   Y   N

I felt more relaxed throughout the day than before this program   Y   N

I felt more relaxed throughout the day than before this program   Y   N

I had less _____ today than before this program

Do THT in the evening. (Check here when done) ☐

Do THT for sleep if necessary.

Notes:

_____

_____

_____

_____

_____

_____

_____

_____

_____

_____

_____

_____

_____

_____

_____

Day 7

I choose my thoughts with care.

Date:_____

I needed THT for Sleep last night Y N

I remembered to use it   Y   N

I slept better than before this program Y N

Do THT in the morning,(Check here when done) ☐ then as needed throughout the day.

Affirmations I used with THT today:

_____

At the end of the day, take a moment to reflect on your day. Was it better than yesterday, the same or worse?_____

I needed to use THT today for

_____

I remembered to use it   Y   N

I felt more relaxed throughout the day than before this program   Y   N

I felt more relaxed throughout the day than before this program   Y   N

I had less _____ today than before this program

Do THT in the evening. (Check here when done) ☐

Do THT for sleep if necessary.

Notes:

_____

_____

_____

_____

_____

_____

_____

_____

_____

_____

_____

_____

_____

_____

Day 8

My mind is like a garden, I can grow weeds, or I can grow flowers.

Date:_____

I needed THT for Sleep last night Y N

I remembered to use it   Y   N

I slept better than before this program Y N

Do THT in the morning,(Check here when done) ☐ then as needed throughout the day.

Affirmations I used with THT today:

_____

At the end of the day, take a moment to reflect on your day. Was it better than yesterday, the same or worse?_____

I needed to use THT today for

_____

I remembered to use it   Y   N

I felt more relaxed throughout the day than before this program   Y   N

I felt more relaxed throughout the day than before this program   Y   N

I had less _____ today than before this program

Do THT in the evening. (Check here when done) ☐

Do THT for sleep if necessary.

Notes:

_____

_____

_____

_____

_____

_____

_____

_____

_____

_____

_____

_____

_____

_____

Day 9

They say that you are what you eat; also you are what you think.

Date:_____

I needed THT for Sleep last night Y N

I remembered to use it   Y   N

I slept better than before this program Y N

Do THT in the morning,(Check here when done) ☐ then as needed throughout the day.

Affirmations I used with THT today:

_____

At the end of the day, take a moment to reflect on your day. Was it better than yesterday, the same or worse?_____

I needed to use THT today for

_____

I remembered to use it   Y   N

I felt more relaxed throughout the day than before this program   Y   N

I felt more relaxed throughout the day than before this program   Y   N

I had less _____ today than before this program

Do THT in the evening. (Check here when done) ☐

Do THT for sleep if necessary.

Notes:

_____

_____

_____

_____

_____

_____

_____

_____

_____

_____

_____

_____

_____

_____

Day 10

I am aware of my thoughts.

Date:_____

I needed THT for Sleep last night Y N

I remembered to use it   Y   N

I slept better than before this program Y N

Do THT in the morning,(Check here when done) ☐ then as needed throughout the day.

Affirmations I used with THT today:

_____

At the end of the day, take a moment to reflect on your day. Was it better than yesterday, the same or worse?_____

I needed to use THT today for

_____

I remembered to use it   Y   N

I felt more relaxed throughout the day than before this program   Y   N

I felt more relaxed throughout the day than before this program   Y   N

I had less _____ today than before this program

Do THT in the evening. (Check here when done) ☐

Do THT for sleep if necessary.

Notes:

_____
_____
_____
_____
_____
_____
_____
_____
_____
_____
_____
_____
_____

Day 11

I choose thoughts that make me feel good.

Date:_____

I needed THT for Sleep last night Y N

I remembered to use it   Y   N

I slept better than before this program Y N

Do THT in the morning,(Check here when done) ☐ then as needed throughout the day.

Affirmations I used with THT today:

_____

At the end of the day, take a moment to reflect on your day. Was it better than yesterday, the same or worse?_____

I needed to use THT today for

_____

I remembered to use it   Y   N

I felt more relaxed throughout the day than before this program   Y   N

I felt more relaxed throughout the day than before this program   Y   N

I had less _____ today than before this program

Do THT in the evening. (Check here when done) ☐

Do THT for sleep if necessary.

Notes:

_____

_____

_____

_____

_____

_____

_____

_____

_____

_____

_____

_____

_____

Day 12

I choose thoughts of gratitude.

Date:_____

I needed THT for Sleep last night Y N

I remembered to use it   Y   N

I slept better than before this program Y N

Do THT in the morning,(Check here when done) ☐ then as needed throughout the day.

Affirmations I used with THT today:

_____

At the end of the day, take a moment to reflect on your day. Was it better than yesterday, the same or worse?_____

I needed to use THT today for

_____

I remembered to use it   Y   N

I felt more relaxed throughout the day than before this program   Y   N

I felt more relaxed throughout the day than before this program   Y   N

I had less _____ today than before this program

Do THT in the evening. (Check here when done) ☐

Do THT for sleep if necessary.

Notes:

_____

_____

_____

_____

_____

_____

_____

_____

_____

_____

_____

_____

_____

_____

Day 13

I am mindful of my thoughts.

Date:_____

I needed THT for Sleep last night Y N

I remembered to use it   Y   N

I slept better than before this program Y N

Do THT in the morning,(Check here when done) ☐ then as needed throughout the day.

Affirmations I used with THT today:

_____

At the end of the day, take a moment to reflect on your day. Was it better than yesterday, the same or worse?_____

I needed to use THT today for

_____

I remembered to use it   Y   N

I felt more relaxed throughout the day than before this program   Y   N

I felt more relaxed throughout the day than before this program   Y   N

I had less _____ today than before this program

Do THT in the evening. (Check here when done) ☐

Do THT for sleep if necessary.

Notes:

_____

_____

_____

_____

_____

_____

_____

_____

_____

_____

_____

_____

_____

_____

_____

Day 14

Thoughts can destroy, or thoughts can create.

Date:_____

I needed THT for Sleep last night Y N

I remembered to use it   Y   N

I slept better than before this program Y N

Do THT in the morning,(Check here when done) ☐ then as needed throughout the day.

Affirmations I used with THT today:

_____

At the end of the day, take a moment to reflect on your day. Was it better than yesterday, the same or worse?_____

I needed to use THT today for

_____

I remembered to use it   Y   N

I felt more relaxed throughout the day than before this program   Y   N

I felt more relaxed throughout the day than before this program   Y   N

I had less _____ today than before this program

Do THT in the evening. (Check here when done) ☐

Do THT for sleep if necessary.

Notes:

_____

_____

_____

_____

_____

_____

_____

_____

_____

_____

_____

_____

_____

Day 15

I choose empowering thoughts.

Date:_____

I needed THT for Sleep last night Y N

I remembered to use it   Y   N

I slept better than before this program Y N

Do THT in the morning,(Check here when done) ☐ then as needed throughout the day.

Affirmations I used with THT today:

_____

At the end of the day, take a moment to reflect on your day. Was it better than yesterday, the same or worse?_____

I needed to use THT today for

_____

I remembered to use it   Y   N

I felt more relaxed throughout the day than before this program   Y   N

I felt more relaxed throughout the day than before this program   Y   N

I had less _____ today than before this program

Do THT in the evening. (Check here when done) ☐

Do THT for sleep if necessary.

Notes:

_____

_____

_____

_____

_____

_____

_____

_____

_____

_____

_____

_____

_____

_____

_____

Day 16

I use my thoughts to create what I want.

Date:_____

I needed THT for Sleep last night Y N

I remembered to use it   Y   N

I slept better than before this program Y N

Do THT in the morning,(Check here when done) ☐ then as needed throughout the day.

Affirmations I used with THT today:

_____

At the end of the day, take a moment to reflect on your day. Was it better than yesterday, the same or worse?_____

I needed to use THT today for

_____

I remembered to use it   Y   N

I felt more relaxed throughout the day than before this program   Y   N

I felt more relaxed throughout the day than before this program   Y   N

I had less _____ today than before this program

Do THT in the evening. (Check here when done) ☐

Do THT for sleep if necessary.

Notes:

_____

_____

_____

_____

_____

_____

_____

_____

_____

_____

_____

_____

_____

_____

_____

Day 17

I focus my thoughts on what I am doing.

Date:_____

I needed THT for Sleep last night Y N

I remembered to use it   Y   N

I slept better than before this program Y N

Do THT in the morning,(Check here when done) ☐ then as needed throughout the day.

Affirmations I used with THT today:

_____

At the end of the day, take a moment to reflect on your day. Was it better than yesterday, the same or worse?_____

I needed to use THT today for

_____

I remembered to use it   Y   N

I felt more relaxed throughout the day than before this program   Y   N

I felt more relaxed throughout the day than before this program   Y   N

I had less _____ today than before this program

Do THT in the evening. (Check here when done) ☐

Do THT for sleep if necessary.

Notes:

_____

_____

_____

_____

_____

_____

_____

_____

_____

_____

_____

_____

_____

_____

Day 18

I don't let my thoughts take me where I don't want to go.

Date:_____

I needed THT for Sleep last night Y N

I remembered to use it   Y   N

I slept better than before this program Y N

Do THT in the morning,(Check here when done) ☐ then as needed throughout the day.

Affirmations I used with THT today:

_____

At the end of the day, take a moment to reflect on your day. Was it better than yesterday, the same or worse?_____

I needed to use THT today for

_____

I remembered to use it   Y   N

I felt more relaxed throughout the day than before this program   Y   N

I felt more relaxed throughout the day than before this program   Y   N

I had less _____ today than before this program

Do THT in the evening. (Check here when done) ☐

Do THT for sleep if necessary.

Notes:

_____
_____
_____
_____
_____
_____
_____
_____
_____
_____
_____
_____
_____
_____
_____

Day 19

I can use my thoughts to practice my talents.

Date:_____

I needed THT for Sleep last night Y N

I remembered to use it   Y   N

I slept better than before this program Y N

Do THT in the morning,(Check here when done) ☐ then as needed throughout the day.

Affirmations I used with THT today:

_____

At the end of the day, take a moment to reflect on your day. Was it better than yesterday, the same or worse?_____

I needed to use THT today for

_____

I remembered to use it   Y   N

I felt more relaxed throughout the day than before this program   Y   N

I felt more relaxed throughout the day than before this program   Y   N

I had less _____ today than before this program

Do THT in the evening. (Check here when done) ☐

Do THT for sleep if necessary.

Notes:

_____

_____

_____

_____

_____

_____

_____

_____

_____

_____

_____

_____

_____

_____

_____

Day 20

I choose how I respond to situations.

Date:_____

I needed THT for Sleep last night Y N

I remembered to use it   Y   N

I slept better than before this program Y N

Do THT in the morning,(Check here when done) ☐ then as needed throughout the day.

Affirmations I used with THT today:

_____

At the end of the day, take a moment to reflect on your day. Was it better than yesterday, the same or worse?_____

I needed to use THT today for

_____

I remembered to use it   Y   N

I felt more relaxed throughout the day than before this program   Y   N

I felt more relaxed throughout the day than before this program   Y   N

I had less _____ today than before this program

Do THT in the evening. (Check here when done) ☐

Do THT for sleep if necessary.

Notes:

_____

_____

_____

_____

_____

_____

_____

_____

_____

_____

_____

_____

_____

Day 21

I don't let what I thought yesterday control what I think today.

Date:_____

I needed THT for Sleep last night Y N

I remembered to use it   Y   N

I slept better than before this program Y N

Do THT in the morning,(Check here when done) ☐ then as needed throughout the day.

Affirmations I used with THT today:

_____

At the end of the day, take a moment to reflect on your day. Was it better than yesterday, the same or worse?_____

I needed to use THT today for

_____

I remembered to use it   Y   N

I felt more relaxed throughout the day than before this program   Y   N

I felt more relaxed throughout the day than before this program   Y   N

I had less _____ today than before this program

Do THT in the evening. (Check here when done) ☐

Do THT for sleep if necessary.

Notes:

_____

_____

_____

_____

_____

_____

_____

_____

_____

_____

_____

_____

_____

_____

Now that you have completed this workbook, please retake this survey so that you can see how things have changed.

Please circle all that apply. I experience:

Anxiety-

Severity: 0   1   2   3   4   5   6   7   8   9   10

Frequency: Daily   Weekly   Monthly   Yearly

Stress-

Severity: 0   1   2   3   4   5   6   7   8   9   10

Frequency: Daily   Weekly   Monthly   Yearly

Depression-

Severity: 0   1   2   3   4   5   6   7   8   9   10

Frequency: Daily   Weekly   Monthly   Yearly

ADHD/ADD-

Severity: 0   1   2   3   4   5   6   7   8   9   10

Frequency: Daily   Weekly   Monthly   Yearly

Phobias/fears-: _____

Severity: 0 1 2 3 4 5 6 7 8 9 10

Frequency: Daily   Weekly   Monthly   Yearly

Insomnia-

Severity: 0 1 2 3 4 5 6 7 8 9 10

Frequency: Daily   Weekly   Monthly   Yearly

Irritability-

Severity: 0 1 2 3 4 5 6 7 8 9 10

Frequency: Daily   Weekly   Monthly   Yearly

Anger-

Severity: 0 1 2 3 4 5 6 7 8 9 10

Frequency: Daily   Weekly   Monthly   Yearly

Obsessive/negative thoughts-

Severity: 0 1 2 3 4 5 6 7 8 9 10

Frequency: Daily   Weekly   Monthly   Yearly

Mental/emotional breakdown-

Severity: 0 1 2 3 4 5 6 7 8 9 10

Frequency: Daily   Weekly   Monthly   Yearly

List of medications I currently take for these issues:

_____

_____

_____

_____

List of medications my doctor reduced or took me off for these issues:

_____

_____

_____

_____

Circle one
I Feel overall happier after doing this program than I did before:

A lot   Somewhat   Not much   None

Thank you for joining me on this journey toward a happier life. I hope that this has helped you and will continue to do so. I would love to read about your stories. You can find my page: facebook.com/twohandstouching

You can watch videos on how to do THT here youtube.com/junipertreeb

You can also connect with me on my website: https://twohandstouching.wordpress.com/

Remember to continue using THT for ongoing benefit. You can also do the Workbook Using EZDS for deeper issues, or the Workbook Using EZAS for a more positive attitude.

Notes:

_____

_____

_____

_____

Notes continued: